Dolphin Freedom for Wally and Molly

Written and Illustrated by Georgie Dolphin

Website: www.freedomfordolphins.com
Email: letdolphinsswimfree@gmail.com

Copyright © 2017 by Georgie Dolphin

The right of Georgie Dolphin to be identified as the author and illustrator of this work has been asserted by her in accordance with the Copyright Acts of 1964 Australia.
All rights reserved. No part of this publication may be reproduced, stored in or introduced into a retrieval system or transmitted, in any form, or by any means (electronic, mechanical, photocopying, recording or otherwise) without the prior written permission of the author.

Sam was a little boy. He was four years old and had loved dolphins ever since he saw some swimming wild and free in the ocean.

His Mummy and Daddy once took him on a boat ride and a huge family, or pod, of dolphins played in the waves of their boat, jumping, diving and splashing in the water.

One of the dolphins caught Sam's eye because it jumped so close to him, so he named it 'Wally the Wild Dolphin'.

Knowing how much Sam loved dolphins, his Mum and Dad were excited to take him to a marine park for his 5th birthday. As they sat in their seats ready to watch the dolphin show they saw 20 dolphins in the concrete pool.

The star of the show, 'Molly the Marine Park Dolphin', had to perform tricks with the other dolphins. They had to bounce balls on their noses and jump through hoops. The show came to a dramatic close as Molly and another dolphin had to push a dolphin trainer up high into the air on their noses.

After the show, Sam went to see 'Molly the Marine Park Dolphin' and he saw the sadness in her eyes. She appeared to be smiling, but Sam had learnt that dolphins cannot 'smile' like we do. Their faces are just shaped that way to help them catch fish.

Molly and the other dolphins were still trapped in the pool, unable to get home to the ocean. Sam saw that keeping dolphins in marine parks made them sad so he went to tell his Mum and Dad. They too could see how terrible Molly's life was compared to Wally's life in the wild, so they all promised Molly that they would help to free her.

Sam thought about Wally and Molly. Wild dolphins swim a long way every day in family pods, diving deep in the ocean, catching fresh fish and squid to eat. Molly was instead trapped in a shallow pool where she could only swim in small circles, made to perform tricks for frozen fish.

Dolphins have very close bonds with their families and care for each other just like we do. 'Wally the Wild Dolphin' had lived with his family in the ocean since he was born, but Molly had been separated from her Mum and they missed each other very much.

The next day Sam told all his friends how sad the captive dolphins were and his Mum wrote letters to try to free them. As more people heard the news, fewer visitors went to the marine park.

By Sam's 6th birthday Molly was on TV because the marine park was forced to close down. The dolphins were set free into a huge sea sanctuary and no longer had to perform tricks for food.

Sam and his family jumped for joy because they had learnt that every dolphin should always live wild and free with their family.

Molly and the other dolphins were later released from the sea sanctuary into the ocean where they all swam free, just like 'Wally the Wild Dolphin'.

In her new ocean home Molly had her first baby, named Hope. They were so happy together. They loved swimming in the ocean with their family pod, wild and free forever!

All dolphins should swim happily, wild and free, and not in captivity

DOLPHIN FACTS:

- Dolphins are one of the world's most intelligent species.
- Like us, dolphins are mammals and they cannot breathe underwater.
- Dolphins come up to the surface and breathe through a blowhole on the top of their head.
- Dolphins make clicking sounds which bounce off an object and cause an echo, telling them the size, shape and location of the object. This is called echolocation.
- Dolphins can hear so well underwater that they can locate an object as small as a pea.
- During the first several weeks of life, a mother dolphin must swim non-stop with her baby riding alongside because they are born without enough body fat to float.

MORE DOLPHIN FACTS:

- Captive dolphins, like Molly, rarely use echolocation because each echo would just bounce off the concrete walls of the pool.
- Unlike us, they are voluntary breathers and have to think about every breath they take.
- When sleeping most wild dolphins keep one eye open, shutting down the opposite side of their brain, taking regular naps throughout the day.
- Dolphins have excellent eyesight and can move each eye independently of the other, allowing them to see more.
- Dolphins have 18-26 pairs of teeth but usually swallow their food whole, and eat 8-15 kilos of food each day.

Wally and Molly say,
"PROTECT OUR OCEAN HOME!"

- Most of the Earth's surface (70%) is covered by water.
- Many animal species live in the ocean including the largest animal in the world, the blue whale.
- We must take care of our oceans and protect the animals that live there. They all live in perfect balance.
- The ocean produces half of the oxygen we breathe.
- Looking after the oceans and keeping them healthy is very important because they are our life support.
- We need healthy oceans full of dolphins, whales, sharks, fish and other marine life to be healthy ourselves.
- We must keep litter and rubbish out of the ocean to protect ourselves and the marine animals who live there.

FUN ACTIVITIES!

Activity 1: Colouring In

The following pages include some fun activities for you to try including colouring in, spot the difference, a maze, join the dots, and more.

See how many you can do!

Colour in this picture of Molly and her baby. Do you remember her baby's name?

Activity 2: Spot the Difference

This blue whale is one of Wally and Molly's ocean friends. Can you find six differences between picture A and picture B?

Did you know...
- Blue whales are the largest animals on Earth measuring up to 30 metres long.
- The tongue of a blue whale weighs as much as a whole elephant.
- The heart of a blue whale can weigh as much as a car.

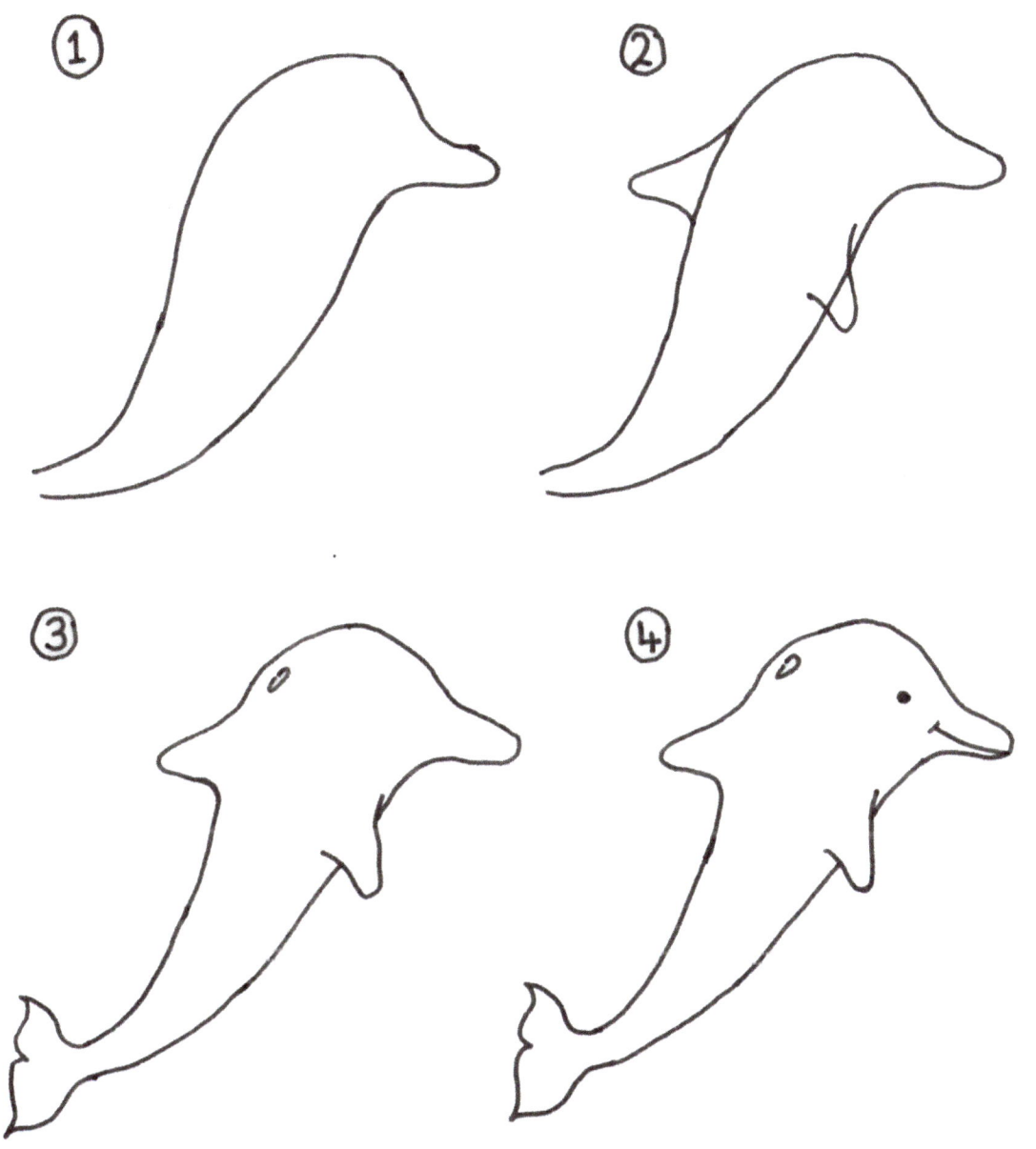

Activity 4: How to draw a dolphin

Activity 5:

Make Your Own 3D Dolphin

Use the template opposite to make your own 3D dolphin just like the example in the photograph!

First, make sure you ask an adult to help you.

Using some card and tracing paper, simply copy the template outline. Then they can carefully cut along the outline and dotted lines so you can attach the tail flukes and insert the flippers through the slit, folding them downwards. You now have your own 3D dolphin!

Activity 6: Join the Dots

Starting at number 1, join up all of the dots in order until you reach number 25. What do you see?

Did you know...
- Great white sharks can grow up to 6 metres long!
- Sharks have gill slits for them to breathe through rather than blowholes like dolphins.
- Many people are scared of sharks, but they do not tend to eat us and attacks are very rare.
- Sharks have more to fear from people who hunt millions of them every year. We need to protect them.

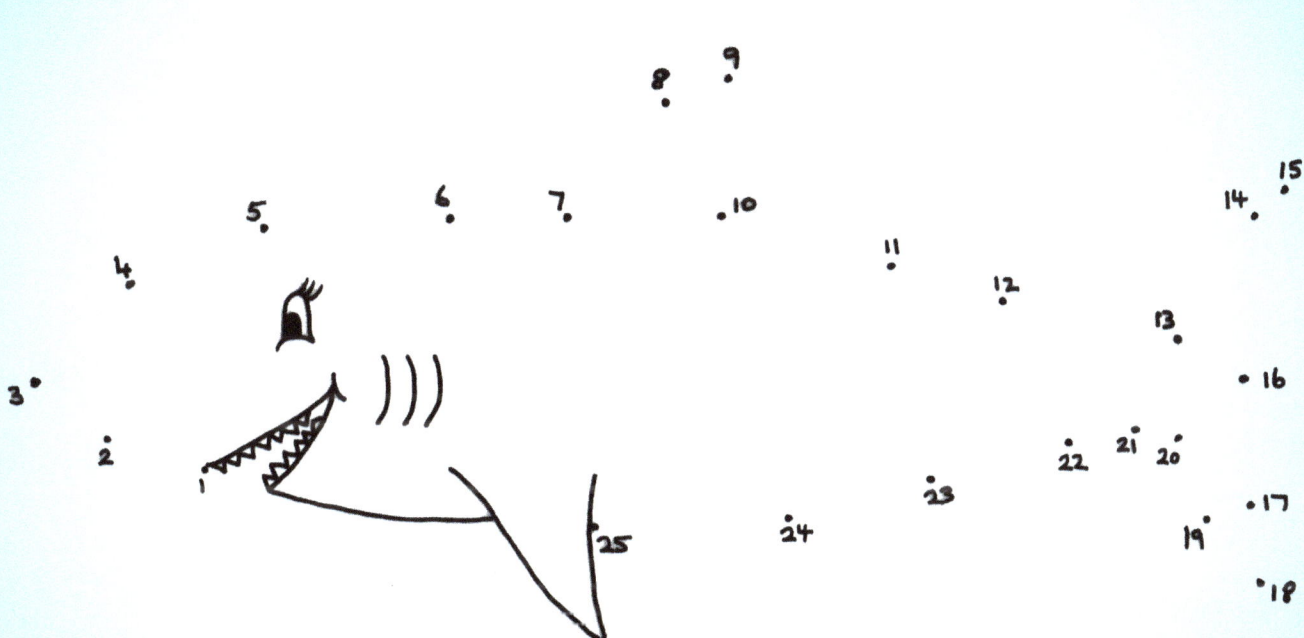

TAKE ACTION TO SAVE DOLPHINS!

Help to save our precious dolphins by colouring in the picture below, then ask an adult to cut along the dotted lines and send it to the Prime Minister of Japan.
TO: Prime Minister of Japan, Cabinet Office, Government of Japan,
1-6-1 Nagata-cho, Chiyoda-ku, Tokyo 100-8914, JAPAN
(Visit www.kantei.go.jp for full contact details).

We are your CHILDREN

We are THE FUTURE

And we LOVE DOLPHINS

Please END DOLPHIN HUNTING and let them live wild and free!

Coloured in by:........................
Age: ....
From (Country):........................

AUTHOR BIOGRAPHY

Georgie Dolphin loves dolphins! She grew up with animals in England and studied Animal Science at Leeds University. After returning to Australia in 2003, Georgie settled in Sydney's northern beaches where she followed her passion for animals and has been working at Humane Society International since 2012. After learning more about captive dolphins from devoted activists and welfare organisations, her determination grew and she set about creating this book. Georgie has shared the story of Wally and Molly with children around the world including in Sydney, China, Singapore and Japan, inspiring them to never go to a dolphin show.

About this Book:

This book was inspired by my beautiful daughter and my amazing Mum, and our shared love of animals. It is dedicated to the dolphins around the world who are living in captivity, and advocating peacefully for their freedom.
By educating our future generations we can create a more empathetic and compassionate world.

www.ingramcontent.com/pod-product-compliance
Lightning Source LLC
Chambersburg PA
CBHW061135010526
44107CB00068B/2949